IN LOVING MEMORY OF JANE BIRKIN

Celebrating the Life of an Extraordinary Artist

Ken Myers

Table of contents

1. Introduction: Remembering Jane Birkin

In the realm of entertainment, certain individuals leave an indelible impression on the hearts and minds of audiences, forever etching their names into the annals of history. Jane Birkin was undeniably one of those extraordinary artists. A British actress, singer, and French icon, Birkin mesmerized audiences around the world with her immense talent, undeniable charm, and distinctive style. As we come together to commemorate her life and legacy, we embark on a journey to remember and honor this remarkable artist.

Born on December 14, 1946, in London, England, Jane Birkin was destined for greatness. She began her artistic journey at a young age, displaying a natural aptitude for both acting and music. Birkin's magnetic presence and versatility quickly propelled her into the spotlight, captivating audiences on both sides of the English Channel.

Birkin's acting career flourished, marked by a series of captivating performances that highlighted her range and depth as a performer. From her early breakthrough roles in films like "Blow-Up" (1966) and "Wonderwall" (1968), to her later collaborations with acclaimed directors such as Jacques Rivette and Agnès Varda, Birkin demonstrated an innate ability to inhabit her characters with authenticity and grace. Her on-screen presence radiated a unique blend of vulnerability, sensuality, and strength, capturing the hearts of viewers around the world.

However, Birkin's artistic pursuits extended far beyond the realm of acting. Collaborating with renowned French musician Serge Gainsbourg, Birkin ventured into the world of music, delivering the unforgettable and controversial hit "Je t'aime... moi non plus" in 1969. This iconic song, with its provocative lyrics and sensual delivery, solidified Birkin's status as a musical sensation and cultural icon.

Apart from her artistic endeavors, Jane Birkin was a symbol of timeless elegance and style. Her effortless and chic fashion sense captivated the fashion world, leading to the creation of the coveted "Birkin Bag" by luxury brand Hermès. Birkin's influence on fashion remains palpable, inspiring designers and fashion lovers alike.

Yet, Birkin's impact extended far beyond the realms of art and fashion. She was a passionate activist, lending her voice and support to environmental causes and various charitable organizations. Birkin's dedication to social issues showcased her compassionate spirit and commitment to making the world a better place.

As we embark on this journey to remember Jane Birkin, we celebrate the life of an extraordinary artist who defied conventions, challenged boundaries, and left an indelible mark on the world. Through her immense talent, timeless elegance, and unwavering dedication to her craft, Birkin's legacy lives on, continuing to inspire and captivate new generations of artists and admirers alike. Join us as we pay tribute to a true icon, reflecting on her enduring spirit and the profound impact she has had on the world of entertainment and beyond.

2. Early Life: From British Roots to French Stardom

Jane Birkin's remarkable journey from her humble beginnings in Britain to becoming a revered icon in France is a testament to her exceptional talent and unwavering determination. This chapter examines her formative years, exploring the influences that shaped her early life and set the stage for her meteoric rise to stardom.

Born on December 14, 1946, in Marylebone, London, Jane Mallory

Birkin was the daughter of Judy Campbell, a renowned actress, and David Birkin, a Royal Navy lieutenant-commander. Growing up in a creative and artistic household, Birkin was exposed to the world of performing arts from an early age. Her mother's influence, in particular, played a significant role in inspiring her passion for acting.

Birkin's education took her to various prestigious institutions, including the independent school, St. Christopher's School in Letchworth. However, her true calling lay in the performing arts, and at the age of 17, she enrolled at the prestigious Drama Centre London, where she honed her acting skills and immersed herself in the craft.

In 1965, at the age of 19, Birkin made her stage debut in the play "The Relapse" at the Oxford Playhouse, marking the beginning of her theatrical journey. Her talent and natural charisma soon caught the attention of filmmakers, leading to her breakthrough in the film industry.

It was during the production of the film "Blow-Up" in 1966 that Birkin caught the eye of French director,

Serge Gainsbourg. This encounter proved to be a pivotal moment in Birkin's life, as it marked the start of a profoundly influential personal and artistic partnership between the two. Gainsbourg recognized Birkin's potential and played a crucial role in introducing her to the French entertainment industry.

Relocating to France, Birkin quickly found success on the silver screen, starring in a string of critically acclaimed French films. Her collaboration with Gainsbourg extended beyond their personal relationship, as they created memorable works together, including the controversial song "Je t'aime... moi non plus," which propelled Birkin to international fame.

Birkin's transition from British actress to French star was seamless, as she effortlessly embraced the French language and culture. Her captivating performances, combined with her enchanting British charm, endeared her to French audiences and solidified her status as a beloved figure in French cinema.

Throughout her early career, Birkin established herself as an actress of immense talent, capable of bringing depth and authenticity to her roles. Her magnetic presence and ability to evoke a range of emotions endeared her to audiences and critics alike, positioning her as one of the most sought-after actresses of her time.

As Jane Birkin embarked on her journey from British roots to French stardom, she not only conquered the film industry but also became a cultural icon and a symbol of cross-cultural artistic collaboration. Her early life experiences and the support she received from her family laid the groundwork for her remarkable success and enduring legacy. In the following chapters, we will explore Birkin's acting career, musical journey, and her profound influence on fashion and style in greater detail.

3. Acting Career: A Journey Through Film and Theater

Jane Birkin's acting career was distinguished by her versatility, depth, and her remarkable ability to captivate viewers with her performances. In this chapter, we will look at the various stages of her acting journey, from her early breakthrough roles to her collaborations with acclaimed directors and her lasting impact on the world of theater and film.

3.1 Rising Star: Breakthrough Roles and Critical Acclaim

Birkin's rise in the acting world began with her breakout role in Michelangelo Antonioni's film "Blow-Up" (1966). Her portrayal of the enigmatic and captivating model, Veruschka, highlighted her talent and drew the attention of critics and audiences alike. The film's international success propelled Birkin into the spotlight and set the stage for a successful career.

Following the success of "Blow-Up," Birkin continued to impress with her performances in films such as "The Knack... and How to Get It" (1965) and "Wonderwall" (1968). Her natural charisma, delicate beauty, and ability to convey complex emotions made her a sought-after actress.

3.2 International Success: Collaborations and Iconic Performances

Birkin's collaboration with renowned French director Jacques Rivette marked a significant turning point in her career. In Rivette's film "La Belle Noiseuse" (1991), she delivered a nuanced and introspective performance that earned her critical acclaim and showcased her range as an actress. The film's success on the international stage further solidified Birkin's reputation as a talent to be reckoned with.

One of Birkin's most memorable performances came in the film "A Soldier's Daughter Never Cries" (1998), directed by James Ivory. Her portrayal of a compassionate and loving mother earned her a nomination for the Golden Globe Award for Best Actress in a Supporting Role. This role exemplified Birkin's ability to bring depth and humanity to her characters, leaving a lasting impression on viewers.

3.3 The Legacy Continues: Birkin's Influence on the Silver Screen

In addition to her own acting accomplishments, Birkin's impact on the film industry extended to her collaborations and influence on subsequent generations of actors and filmmakers. Her unique blend of vulnerability, sensuality, and authenticity continues to inspire artists around the world.

Birkin's commitment to portraying complex female characters with depth and sensitivity paved the way for a new era of storytelling on the silver screen. Her willingness to take on challenging roles and explore the human experience in all its intricacies secured her status as an actress of immense talent and substance.

Throughout her acting career, Jane Birkin demonstrated an unwavering dedication to her craft and a profound understanding of the human condition. Her performances continue to resonate with audiences, and her influence on the world of film remains. In the next chapter, we will delve into Birkin's musical journey, exploring her collaborations with Serge Gainsbourg and her evolution as a musician.

4. Musical Journey: From 'Je t'aime... moi non plus' to Musical Exploration

Jane Birkin's musical journey is an essential part of her artistic legacy. Through her collaboration with renowned musician Serge Gainsbourg, Birkin achieved international fame with the provocative and sensuous hit "Je t'aime... moi non plus." This chapter examines her musical evolution, her collaborations, and her exploration of various musical genres.

4.1 The Notable Duo: Birkin and Serge Gainsbourg

The partnership between Jane Birkin and Serge Gainsbourg was a powerful force that left an indelible mark on the music industry. Their collaboration began with the iconic duet "Je t'aime... moi non plus" in 1969. The song, with its explicit lyrics and sensual delivery, caused a stir but also propelled Birkin into the spotlight.

The chemistry between Birkin and Gainsbourg extended beyond the recording studio. Their real-life romance and artistic collaboration captivated the public's imagination, becoming the subject of fascination and admiration. Together, they pushed boundaries and challenged societal norms, leaving an enduring legacy in the realm of music.

4.2 Solo Career: Birkin's Musical Evolution and Artistic Expression

While Birkin's collaboration with Gainsbourg brought her initial recognition, she embarked on a solo career that showcased her individuality and musical prowess. Her solo albums demonstrated a willingness to explore diverse musical styles and experiment with different sounds.

Birkin's repertoire extended beyond the provocative tunes she had become known for. She delved into folk-inspired melodies, melancholic ballads, and even ventured into world music influences. With each release, Birkin revealed new facets of her artistic expression and further solidified her status as a multifaceted artist.

4.3 Unforgettable Songs: A Discography of Jane Birkin

Throughout her musical career, Birkin released a range of albums that showcased her unique voice and musical sensibilities. Notable albums include "Di Doo Dah" (1973), "Baby Alone in Babylone" (1983), and "Lost Song" (1998). Each album bore the distinct mark of Birkin's artistry, featuring heartfelt performances and evocative lyrics.

Among Birkin's most memorable songs are "Ex-Fan des Sixties,"

"Quoi," and "La Javanaise." These songs not only showcased her vocal abilities but also highlighted her talent for storytelling through music. Birkin's ability to convey emotions with authenticity and vulnerability resonated with listeners and solidified her status as a musical icon.

In her musical exploration, Birkin demonstrated a fearlessness to step outside her comfort zone, collaborating with diverse artists and experimenting with new sounds. Her ability to reinvent herself and embrace new musical horizons cemented her reputation as an artist unafraid of pushing boundaries and challenging expectations.

Jane Birkin's musical journey is an integral part of her artistic legacy. From the provocative duets with Serge Gainsbourg to her solo endeavors and exploration of various genres, Birkin's contribution to the world of music is a testament to her creativity and willingness to forge her own path. In the following chapter, we explore Birkin's impact on fashion and style, as she became a timeless icon of elegance and fashion inspiration.

5. Fashion and Style: Birkin's Timeless Elegance

Jane Birkin's influence extended far beyond the realms of acting and music. Her effortless sense of style and iconic fashion choices made her a timeless symbol of elegance and a source of inspiration for generations. This chapter examines Birkin's impact on fashion, her signature looks, and her lasting legacy as a style icon.

5.1 The Birkin Bag: A Fashion Icon is Born

One of the most iconic contributions Jane Birkin made to the fashion world was the creation of the renowned Birkin Bag. The story goes that during a flight, Birkin happened to sit next to Hermès CEO Jean-Louis Dumas, and as she expressed her dissatisfaction with the lack of practical yet stylish handbags, the idea for the Birkin Bag was born. This encounter led to the design of the now-iconic handbag, which quickly became synonymous with luxury and exclusivity.

The Birkin Bag, characterized by its exquisite craftsmanship, timeless design, and high-quality materials, has achieved legendary status in the world of fashion. Its allure and rarity have made it a sought-after item, with long waiting lists and an enduring status as a symbol of prestige and style.

5.2 Fashion Collaborations and Influences

Birkin's impact on fashion extended beyond the creation of the Birkin Bag. Her personal style, characterized by a combination of simplicity, femininity, and a touch of bohemian charm, captured the attention of designers and fashion enthusiasts worldwide.

Her collaborations with influential designers such as Yves Saint Laurent and Paco Rabanne further solidified her status as a fashion icon. Birkin's natural beauty and innate sense of style made her an ideal muse for designers seeking to channel her effortless elegance and nonchalant glamor into their collections.

Birkin's distinctive fashion choices, which often included classic pieces such as tailored blazers, simple blouses, and high-waisted jeans, continue to inspire fashion trends to this day. Her ability to effortlessly combine comfort and sophistication has made her a timeless reference point for those seeking a sense of effortless chic.

5.3 Jane Birkin's Enduring Impact on Style

Jane Birkin's influence on fashion and style is not limited to a specific era but spans across generations. Her ability to create an aesthetic that seamlessly blended British refinement with French nonchalance remains as pertinent today as it was during her heyday.

Her influence can be seen in the wardrobes of countless individuals, from celebrities to fashion enthusiasts who continue to emulate her iconic looks. The combination of Birkin's natural beauty, bohemian spirit, and timeless elegance serves as a constant source of inspiration, reaffirming her status as a true fashion icon.

Jane Birkin's lasting impact on fashion and style lies in her ability to exude an effortless charm and capture the essence of chic sophistication. Her legacy continues to shape the fashion landscape, serving as a reminder that true style transcends trends and remains eternally relevant. In the following chapter, we explore Birkin's activism and humanitarian work, revealing her commitment to making a positive impact on the world.

6. Activism and Humanitarian Work: Birkin's Commitment to Social Causes

Jane Birkin's influence transcends her artistic accomplishments, as she devoted herself to a variety of social causes, promoting activism and humanitarian efforts. This chapter examines Birkin's commitment to making a positive impact on the world, emphasizing her environmental activism and participation in charitable organizations.

6.1 Environmental Activism: Birkin's Contributions to Protecting the Planet

Birkin's deep concern for the environment drove her to actively engage in environmental activism. She raised awareness about issues such as deforestation, climate change, and the importance of sustainable living. Birkin's enthusiasm for preserving the planet's natural resources motivated her to take action and motivate others to do the same.

Her collaboration with Greenpeace, a global environmental organization, brought attention to various environmental campaigns. Birkin used her platform and influence to advocate for responsible consumption, the protection of endangered species, and the need for renewable energy sources. Her voice resonated with fans and activists worldwide, helping to drive positive change.

6.2 Humanitarian Work: Birkin's Involvement in Charitable Organizations

Birkin's humanitarian efforts extended to her involvement with charitable organizations. She actively supported causes related to children's welfare, healthcare, and education. Birkin's compassion and desire to improve the lives of others led her to work with organizations such as Amnesty International, UNICEF, and the Red Cross.

Her dedication to improving the lives of disadvantaged children and advocating for their rights was particularly noteworthy. Birkin participated in projects focused on providing access to education, healthcare, and essential resources for children in need. Her tireless efforts to make a difference had a profound effect on the lives of countless individuals and communities.

Through her activism and humanitarian work, Birkin demonstrated a deep sense of social responsibility and a desire to use her platform for the betterment of society. Her passion and commitment to causes she believed in inspired others to take action and contribute to positive change.

Jane Birkin's legacy as an artist goes beyond her artistic accomplishments. Her activism and humanitarian work demonstrate her dedication to making a difference in the world. Through her environmental advocacy and involvement in charitable organizations, Birkin leaves a lasting legacy of compassion, empathy, and the belief that each individual has the power to create positive change.

In the final chapter, we reflect on Birkin's personal life, exploring her relationships, motherhood, and the profound impact she had on those closest to her.

7. Contribution to Charitable Organizations Personal Life: Love, Loss, and Motherhood

Behind the illustrious career of Jane Birkin lies a complex personal life, full of love, sorrow, and the joys of motherhood. This chapter examines the significant relationships in Birkin's life, her experiences as a mother, and the profound effect she had on those closest to her.

7.1 Connections and Romances

Jane Birkin's romantic life was characterized by a series of significant relationships that shaped her personal and artistic journey. Her most renowned romance was with the renowned musician Serge Gainsbourg, with whom she had a passionate and tumultuous relationship. Their artistic collaborations and personal bond created a lasting impression on both their lives.

After her separation from Gainsbourg, Birkin continued to explore love and companionship. She had relationships with people such as Jacques Doillon, the father of her daughter, and director and screenwriter John Barry. Each relationship brought its own joys and difficulties, influencing Birkin's personal growth and artistic expression.

7.2 Birkin as a Mother: Her Bond with Her Children

Motherhood was a major part of Jane Birkin's life. She had three daughters—Kate Barry, Charlotte Gainsbourg, and Lou Doillon—and her love for her children was a driving force in her personal and creative endeavors. Birkin's deep devotion and nurturing spirit as a mother fostered strong bonds with her daughters, who would go on to make their own mark in the world of arts and entertainment.

Birkin's relationship with her daughters was one of love, support, and artistic collaboration. She not only provided them with guidance and encouragement but also shared the spotlight with them on various occasions, showcasing their talents and fostering their artistic growth.

7.3 Navigating Loss and Personal Challenges

Throughout her life, Jane Birkin faced personal challenges and the profound pain of loss. The tragic death of her eldest daughter, Kate Barry, in 2013 was a devastating blow that profoundly affected Birkin and her entire family. Birkin's resilience in the face of this loss is a testament to her strength and the deep love she held for her children.

Despite the personal struggles she encountered, Birkin continued to find solace and inspiration in her artistic pursuits, using her creativity as a means of healing and expression. Her capacity to channel her emotions into her work and maintain a sense of grace during difficult times is a testament to her resilience and determination.

The personal life of Jane Birkin, marked by love, sorrow, and the joys of motherhood, added complexity to her journey as an artist. Her relationships and experiences shaped her as a person, influencing her work and leaving a lasting impact on those who had the privilege of knowing her. In the concluding chapter, we reflect on the enduring legacy of Jane Birkin, celebrating her contributions to the arts and the profound influence she continues to have on contemporary culture.

8. The Jane Birkin Legacy: Remembering Her Impact

Jane Birkin's legacy is one of immense talent, artistic exploration, and a profound influence on the worlds of acting, music, fashion, and activism. This final chapter reflects on the lasting legacy she has left behind, honoring her contributions to the arts and the profound effect she continues to have on modern culture.

8.1 Impact on Contemporary Artists and Performers

Jane Birkin's artistic legacy continues to motivate and affect contemporary artists and performers. Her unique combination of vulnerability, sensuality, and genuineness remains a benchmark for those looking to infuse their work with profundity and emotional resonance. Birkin's capacity to captivate audiences with her performances, both on screen and on stage, has set a standard of excellence that artists strive to attain.

Musically, Birkin's collaborations with Serge Gainsbourg and her solo work have left an indelible mark on the music industry. Her exploration of diverse musical genres and her willingness to experiment with new sounds have paved the way for artists to push boundaries and redefine genres.

8.2 Tributes and Fond Memories from the Entertainment Industry

The impact of Jane Birkin's artistic contributions is evident through the tributes and fond memories shared by those who worked with her and were touched by her presence. Fellow actors, musicians, and industry professionals have praised her talent, authenticity, and generous spirit.

Birkin's iconic status in the world of fashion is perpetuated through ongoing collaborations, her influence on design, and the enduring popularity of the Birkin Bag. Fashion designers and enthusiasts continue to draw inspiration from her timeless elegance, which serves as a constant reminder of her lasting impact on style.

8.3 A Cultural Icon and Symbol of Feminine Liberation

Jane Birkin's cultural significance extends beyond her artistic achievements. She became a symbol of feminine liberation and challenged societal norms through her bold choices and refusal to conform to expectations. Her unapologetic embrace of her sensuality and her fearless exploration of love and desire through her work paved the way for greater artistic freedom and expression.

Birkin's advocacy for environmental causes and her involvement in charitable organizations showcased her commitment to making a positive impact on the world. Her activism serves as a reminder of the importance of using one's platform to drive change and motivate others to take action.

In conclusion, Jane Birkin's legacy as an extraordinary artist, style icon, and humanitarian is one that continues to reverberate and inspire. Her contributions to the arts, her timeless elegance, and her unwavering commitment to social causes have left an indelible mark on the world. Through her work and the effect she had on those around her, Birkin remains a beacon of creativity, authenticity, and resilience. As we remember and celebrate her life, we recognize the lasting legacy she has left behind, forever inscribing her name in the annals of artistic greatness.

www.ingramcontent.com/pod-product-compliance
Ingram Content Group UK Ltd.
Pitfield, Milton Keynes, MK11 3LW, UK
UKHW022007190726
13853UKWH00004B/1788

9 798852 609595